From the Inside Quietly

ELOISA AMEZCUA

SHELTERBELT PRESS

Published by Shelterbelt Press

Springfield, Illinois 62703

www.shelterbeltpress.org

Cover Art & Layout: Brytton Bjorngaard

ISBN: 978-0-692-95548-2

To my parents. Con amor.

"The way you hold something in you matters."

- Joanna Klink

TABLE OF CONTENTS

E DOES BALLET

little-bodied in a pink tutu
and matching leotard

a mirrored room

chubby mother says
when comparing her

to the other girls

but she's due for a growth
spurt this summer

the bottom of the pool

opal and shimmering
broken glass sealed in stone

smooth against her feet

she wears sunscreen like talc
on sunburned cheeks

chlorine water rushes

into her mouth as she sinks
legs akimbo to the pool floor

screaming words she shouldn't know

TEACHING MY MOTHER ENGLISH OVER THE PHONE

I try to explain the difference   between pant and pants
why the former isn't simply   one pair

but what the lungs do   with fear or excitement
why clothe isn't a singular noun

but what most do to the body   each morning
she calls on a Wednesday   needs help

with an assignment   for her third English
beginners course where she meets   twice a week

her classmates from countries   with names beautiful as hers
I try to make the language   clear to my mother

as she one day   —before my English took hold—
explained to me that   I did not in fact make friends

      with a girl named Sorry

but we were on the playground and she hit me, fue accidenté,
y me dijo "I'm sorry" and when someone says I am, yo soy—

that's not how this works I remind her

when she asks   if the plural of dust is dusts
she asks me to conjugate   love

I love you   love he loves   she loved
we loved you   have loved   I am loving

she wants to know how   a word can be both
a thing and an action   like war and mistake

although I can't put into words in Spanish
how I know the difference   so I tell her I have to go

and I go   and she goes   I haven't taught her anything

THERE WAS NOTHING TO DO BUT HURT
EACH OTHER IN A PLACE LIKE THAT

We drive the back roads deeper
into the desert. We've driven

this road before, alone together.
Mother tells me about the house

built by her father on the outskirts
of San Luis Río Colorado,

how garbage trucks didn't make it
that far from town so the family burned

trash in a pit out back every night.
The useless pile's glow visible for miles.

She tells me about her siblings—
five sisters, two brothers—

how they threw her in that pit
one morning. They called her pollita

and cenicienta, her fair skin ashen
and filthy. *They hated me*, she says,

we hated each other. She blames
her hair—the light strands

in old photographs surrounded
by manes black like mine. *I brushed it*

obsessively, mother tells me. *Hundreds*
of times a night, she says. The sun

peaks over the Sand Tank Mountains.
Her blonde hair turns white nearly.

It's been years since I've touched it.
The smell of dirt and sun seeps in

through vents, mixes with the cool
air keeping us awake. I count saguaros,

imagine sitting under their long shadows.
But they pass too quickly or I give up

too easily. We drive and mother tells me
about the time she ran from one end

of the hallway to the other, leapfrogging
over her sister who sat on the floor

cutting paper dresses for her paper dolls.
Tia Imelda stabbed her in the knee

with a pair of dull scissors. And mother
hesitates to tell me what her sister

yelled before thrusting
the rusted blades into her small body:

You do that one more time and I'll kill you.

HER WANT OF IT

my sister got
a handgun
for her birthday

my brother-in-law
bought my sister
a handgun

for her birthday
I won't stay over
at your house

anymore I say
we argue over
her need of it

what if someone
breaks into the house
what if someone

pulls a gun on me
I remind her
she has two

children I remind
her we are not
the shooting type

what if a deranged
someone tries to hurt
me or my family

I remind her
she'd have to
pull the trigger

we argue over
her want of it
I'll use the gun

safely she says
I remind her
what safe means

I send her news
clippings of mass
shootings I send

her statistics
and charts with
y-access numbers

in the tens
of thousands
I tell her I love her

when she sends
me a picture of
the pink pistol

isn't it cute?

INCIDENT

kitchen dimly lit   by the streetlamp   outside

behind my eyes   flashes of static   call it loss

look for memories   I don't remember   a thing

the table brown   think harder   the tile

too clean for   the mess   I made

my incident   sitting in a swamp   of my own piss

heartbeat too fast   for my body   syncope

a memory   I'm tired of falling   again and again

PSYCHIATRIST'S DAUGHTER

There's talk of tragedy
on the local news

one room over. "Here is
a person who was living

and is now dead,"
the anchor says

with no inflection. My father
tells me about this patient

over dinner. How
she was murdered,

beaten in a dusty backstreet
not far from where

we live. "She has the same
birthday as your sister,"

he says. She had a father
who was not my father,

who did not know her
the way my father does,

I think when he says this.
He takes another bite.

/

It's not unusual
to discuss the dead

at our table. Father
explains how red

the insides of bodies
are, where he was

the first time he peeled
skin and fascia to reveal

muscle, the names of bones
pulled from stranger's bodies.

/

I ask him her name.
He won't tell, doesn't

have to. The red banner
scrolls across the TV

screen. Police name her,
ID 17-year-old

girl found dead in alley.
I thought I'd heard her name

before, but I don't know
this girl the way my father does.

He sits still at the dinner table
preparing other patients'

progress notes for another
day's work. But her body

is on display as news.
A "chronic runaway."

The police promise
they're working backwards

to find her killer.

ON WANTING TO BE MORE ECO-FRIENDLY

I tell my lover I want to be buried
in a mushroom suit and he looks at me

the way you look at someone who's
just told you they'd like to be buried

in a mushroom suit. I'm looking for a greener
way to go, I say as we sip diner coffee

from Styrofoam cups. I explain how
the body becomes food for the fungi,

describe the cremini and shiitake's
capacity to digest fat and flesh. He says

it's morbid to discuss this over eggs
benedict, and besides, wouldn't animals

ravage the corpse, separate ulna
from radius, chew through tissue

to knucklebones and kneecaps
before it can fully decompose?

I guess he has a point. Still, I tell him,
the truth is you'll leave the world a corpse

swallowed by formaldehyde or fire
or dirt. Heavy metals—lead and mercury—

leaking from stiff pores into soil
and groundwater, forming smoke clouds

overhead. We're literally toxic, I tell him.
I'd rather become compost:

food and dead and shit and half-eaten.

TEXACO, TEXACO

With eyes closed, I pictured different boys
from school and TV, practiced kissing them

on my arm in the third row of our family SUV.
I listened to Destiny's Child and *NSYNC

on my portable CD player—a Casio.
My parents thought I was asleep as I slipped

my tongue slowly in and out of my mouth.
I was good at this. I was ready

for the real thing. I was eleven
and headed to San Luis for Nana's 65th birthday,

and I knew American eleven meant Mexican thirteen
so if the older neighborhood boys came to the party

I'd kiss them and they'd say, *Wow, you're good at that*.
And I'd know those five hours in the car—

the stop at the gas station in Gila Bend
and again in Yuma, when the neon light

filtering in through tinted windows turned
everything redder, more serious, when I stayed

in the backseat with the luggage and groceries
and pretended to sleep, drool and spit covering

pinkish bruises at the crook of my elbow—
they meant something:

I was good.
I knew it.
I was a natural.

LONG DISTANCE

I tried touching myself
   but was too disgusted
to finish because my hand
   isn't your hand.
My friend, the virgin, calls this
   love. I can't look
at my reflection and see
   more than poor muscle
definition and dimpling of thighs
   without you here
to tell me it's all in my mind.
   A housewife, like my mother,
would call this love.
   I teach you Spanish
over the phone
   calling that love, patient
when you confuse mouth
   with tongue. You remember
nervio is nerve and lemon,
   limón—those are easy.
But toronja is grapefruit,
   not Toronto, and flema

does not mean flame. I keep

      certain words from you

because I, too, wish

      it were simpler. That dispara

were despair, and lobo

      lobster, amor

armor. But sound

      does not translate meaning—

panocha is not Pandora,

      although both are woman

and you are far.

E GOES TO THE MUSEUM

she finds the term *natural*
history problematic

taxidermic animals
giraffes and sea turtles

with Linnaean names
       phylum   *order*   *family*   *genus*

a wall of venomous snakes
their fangs and jaws labeled

the shark teeth tell stories
she wants to learn by heart

two zebra finches starved
by the window in the kitchen

a family gone for the weekend
and the girl seven years old

forgot to feed them
        she pulled the dead things

from their cage   held white-bellied
birds in small hands

children and parents spill out
of the entrance

the world knows of her
what she does not know of herself

SHE

Not dumb, but not the smartest. Not ugly, but not drop-dead
gorgeous. Not clumsy, but not graceful. Not naïve, but not
worldly. Not oblivious, but not quick. Not a bad dancer,
but not a good ballerina. Not stiff, but not as supple
as the rest. Not fat, but not thin enough. Not dark, but not
light enough. Not dumb, but not the smartest. Not fake,
but not genuine. Not warm, but not cold either.
Not smiling, but not frowning. Not slutty, but not prudish. Not
a virgin, but not a whore. Not easy, but not unwilling. Not staying,
but not leaving. Not taking, but not giving. Not hurt, but
not unharmed. Not tall, but not short. Not used, but not
untouched. Not carefree, but not concerned. Not scared,
but not at ease. Not plain, but not flashy. Not ugly, but
not drop-dead gorgeous. Not happy, but not sad. Not
a person, but a body is she.

FRIDAY NIGHT AT A SWEDISH HARD ROCK CONCERT

Cambridge, Massachusetts

All the white,
bearded dudes bob

their heads in unison.
Junkies nod off

and the four men
on stage with umlauted

last names look like
replicas of each other:

long blonde hair,
mustaches, tight

jeans, and sweaty shirts.
I think of your face,

your chin resting on top
of my black-brown cropped

cut. I can't remember
if your hair falls over

your left or right eye.
You could be Swedish too.

I remember the first time
you heard me speak

Spanish on the phone
with my mother. You

smiled at the change
in my tone. You didn't

know I was serious
when I told you

I grew up listening
to cumbias and Café

Tacuba. Tonight, we stand
close to the speakers—

your favorite spot
off to the side.

The lead singer's vowels
vibrate in my ears.

I watch the moshing
in the center of the room.

A man lets another
punch him in the face.

I guess everybody's
just trying to feel something

or someone. The woman
to our left watches

the show through her iPhone.
You go to the bar and I go

to the bathroom and I don't
hear you yell my four-syllable

name the *like ten times*
you say you did. But

I believe you like I believe
the buzzing in my ears

may never go away. And
we leave, tired but whole.

AFTER SYLVIA PLATH

how can anyone write about bees

but because the bathroom fan at the motel
        in Killington buzzes

the constant hum while I shower

I face the faucet
        my fear my fear my fear

a swarm will come and it does
every drop stings   I have no protection

little bees melt into this body
reddening

the iron smell of water like blood
fills my nostrils and drink

yes
        I drink

savage mouthfuls   tiny creatures
slice my throat

I swallow   lather
splattered insects and scentless soap

from my ugly wrists to torso
he waits outside the locked door

a pressed shirt
        another wedding   another suit

grey water pools past itchy ankles
I open my mouth spit out

the progeny the wings

ON NOT SCREAMING

I told you
to be quiet,
he said,
is to love
me enough
to let me in—

/

I imagine that's what
a man says to the child
he's going to take if he's
in the business of taking
children.

/

If a man tried to take
me he wouldn't know that
I don't know how to scream,
haven't heard what sound
would come out if I tried.

/

I was small
when a boy
only a few
years older
ripped a dollar
from my hand
at the fair.
It was my toll
for the caterpillar ride.
He looked hungry
and told me *Shhhhh*
as he walked away.
I didn't tell
my older sister
till it was our turn
to climb in
and the operator asked
for our fare—
we were short.
I waited for her
near the exit.
She told me
not to tell
mom or dad.
They'd worry,
and anyways
I was fine
with being quiet.

/

This is how I was
taught to love:
to silence yourself
is to let the other in.

MY MOTHER'S BEEN TRYING TO KILL ME SINCE THE DAY I WAS BORN

clinging umbilical
and needy I lay
in a puddle dim
and shallow inside
my mother
a different cold
choking on her
body my noose
she pushed and
strangled me
further into
herself
until doctors
incised through
layers of her
womanhood
gloved hands
pulled me
bruise-colored
out of the womb
alive and furious

BOY,

they say you should not remove
foreign objects from the body for fear
it will bleed out, but you entered
and removed and re-entered
and re-moved yourself
as if trying to make me live,
or else. There comes
a time when, just to feel,
a girl will put anything
between her legs.

CAR TALK

Peggy calls in. She's
looking for a man,

wants to put out an ad
for a car she doesn't own.

We listen
on another ride

home. She can date
the prospective buyer,

she says, needs help
deciding what car

would attract the right
person. Kind, funny,

adventurous. The way
we describe each other

to strangers.
Tom and Ray think

it's a great idea, a 1959
Land Rover. We listen

closely, don't want to say
the wrong thing

after a night of arguing.
Say you brought it back

from Kenya. Say you were
on a safari. We laugh.

Say you'd hate to part
with the car

when he comes to check
it out. Say it's a lie,

that you're looking
for a man. Say you feel

bad for Peggy,
you hope she finds

what she deserves. Tom
and Ray say to put out

a wanted ad for the car
instead. Driver included.

Say something before
the next caller.

I think we mean
to say we're sorry.

When our small mouths
open, we sigh.

K,

I saw your ex, the most recent,
the one you loved, yesterday

walking down the street. He was
with another man, hair shiny

and black like yours. Your old love,
he looked thinner, almost hungry.

I wanted to take a picture. Text it to you.
Tell you that I miss when you lived

in this city. Tell you that D and I
switched sides of the bed last night.

It was my idea. I woke confused
and lost and was tired at work all day

yesterday. When I saw your ex
from my car at the corner of Portland

and Broadway, I thought of the Halloween
party at G's fourth-floor apartment

overlooking the cemetery. You were
dressed as Salvador Dali and I wore

a flapper's dress and strands of faux-pearls.
We were obsessed with Russian poets and men

that didn't know us and mostly each other.
You told me that falling in love

with someone new was just falling
in love with yourself over and over again.

We knew then that nothing hurts
as bad as nothing feels.

CANDIDA

I consider putting cold yogurt in my second mouth.
A website called Home Remedies for Life says this can mend
a yeast infection but the uneaten tub of Chobani expired
yesterday. I read a woman made sourdough bread using yeast
from her vagina and the loaf rose but wasn't tangy
the way sourdough is supposed to be. I'd like to swallow
a part of my body, to cannibalize myself into myself—
maybe I'd have thicker hair and thin wrists, delicate.
I say delicate but mean clean, mean unblemished.
A cigarette burn on the right, scar faded
on the left. As a child, I learned to bathe myself
in my parent's shower. I stepped onto the ledge
meant for propping one's foot to shave or for sex,
reached for the soap and slipped, my wrist gashed
open from my father's razor. I yelled for my mother
who thought it was shampoo in my eyes
again. She shouted to rinse it out with water. I yelled
blood, kept yelling and she came to put me back together.
She put me back together. My lover asks
if I want to sit on his face, if I want his mouth
to eat my mouth that doesn't eat and I tell him no.
Tell him I can feel my vulva pulsing with heat
but not in the way he wishes. I reach my hand
into black cotton panties, the lace collecting dust
in a drawer. I'm swollen. I don't have to look
to know it's red. And again I blame my mother.
I didn't come out of her vagina but still she's an exit
wound and I'm the bullet, or the gun, or the bullet and the gun.

DEFENESTRATION

Have I told you about cats
falling from windows?

How the lower the window,
the more damage to the body;

the more room they have
to fall, the more they can catch

themselves on the way down.
Who hasn't fallen in love

and wished to swing their head,
arch their back, splay legs

like wings and land on their feet?
I fell once, from an airplane,

on purpose. I didn't love the man
strapped to my back but for a moment

I might have. He asked if I
was alright when I fell silent

as we tumbled toward earth
like a comet. I was excited,

I swear. It's just that I had already
fallen, and I knew the difference

between falling out of control
and falling into it. Love, I turn

to you on nights so purple
so dark as my muscles loosen

and hands uncurl because I don't know
the difference between what will happen

and why it happens. Still, we fall asleep
and there is no more falling, just me

and you in this first-floor cat-less apartment.

E WALKS HOME ALONE:
AN INNER MONOLOGUE

map your surroundings

locate another woman   locate

a group of women   locate a well-lit space

        to stop and punch

9-1-1 into your cellphone   if needed

hold your cellphone   hold your thumb

over the green 'dial' button   hold

        your cellphone inside a pocket

your keys in the other

head between two fingers   blade sticking

out from your fist like a small rhinoceros

        [whose only predator is man]

wear clothing with pockets   wear nothing

that clings to your shape   be shapeless

don't look scaredworriedpanicked   don't look

friendlyapproachableopen   don't look back

        look natural

don't smile   don't not smile   don't

come undone   the key is to go unnoticed

the key is to get where you're going

the key is to hold yourself

inside of yourself as long as you can

FAINT

verb

1. to lose consciousness for a short period of time because of a temporarily insufficient supply of oxygen to the brain

   as in:

I fainted. I faint.

   as in:

The first time I fainted was in second grade on the concrete basketball court during PE. Then in the shower. Then coming down the stairs. Then at the doctor's office when it was on purpose. He slipped nitroglycerin under my tongue to see what would happen. I stood strapped at a ninety-degree angle perpendicular to the floor, the rough bands left marks on my arms for hours after. Then. Then. Then while you slept in our bed one room over and I woke you and said I fainted. You looked scared and put ice on the back of my head. Syncope the doctor said. *Concussion.*

2. [archaic] to grow weak or feeble; decline

   as in:

I know it can seem at times like our love is fainting. You kiss my neck, place a hand on my thigh and I cringe, stiffen—a reflex. I'm sorry, I'm not used to this vulnerability, this being so open to falling.

adjective

1. barely perceptible

   as in:

Sometimes when I wake, the faint smell of last night's dinner lingers in stale air, my small apartment, the Craigslist couch. You're a good cook, and patient. You reach a hand to pull gizzards and organs from a small pack inside the chicken, run water over tender flesh. Slowly you peel vegetables. Sweet potato skin falls faint on the linoleum countertop.

as in:

I lie in bed pretending to sleep. I hear the faint murmurs of your dreaming-self beside me. I make out *don'ts* and *waits*.

2. *slight or remote*

as in:

There's a faint chance that I'll leave you today. There's a thing in me that wants out, needs to flee the world, this body.

as in:

The likelihood that this will happen is faint.

3. *lacking in strength or enthusiasm*

as in:

The faint beat of my heart scares you sometimes. You think it's a metaphor but the doctors blame my brain, my blood, its volume. The faint sympathies of the nervous system.

4. *[predict.] weak and dizzy; close to losing consciousness*

as in:

I feel faint in the morning when I wake. I feel faint when I get up from the toilet. I feel faint after eating, before I wash the dishes, as I brush my teeth. I feel faint while making love. I feel faint when I look in the mirror at my worn-out limbs and aching chest. I feel faint on Tuesdays and Wednesdays and Thursdays. I feel faint as I take my medicine: 80mg 1x/day, 60mg 3x/day, 290mcg 1x/day, 50mg as needed.

noun

1. *a sudden loss of consciousness*

        as in:

In a dead faint I fall to the floor.

SIDE-IMPACT

I call you Saturday night
after the accident, collect

shards of glass from my comforter.
I shouldn't have laid down

when I got home but I was so tired.
I want to tell you about the other

driver's face, how pale and stiff
she looked, how a man knocked

on the window of the borrowed
pickup I'd been driving. He asked

if I was alright as the streetlights
changed from green to yellow

and cars passed us though the truck
was facing the direction I'd come from.

Police showed up, the samaritan who'd
come to my window gave a statement

using words like T-bone and too fast.
His dark hands moved slow. I his left,

the other driver his right meeting
at the intersection, the center of his body

in a crash. My father came to get me
in mother's car. And the woman

was unconscious like it was my fault
she ran the red light. Medics worked

to free her and still—her neck
stretched out, eyes closed, mouth open.

The face jagged and familiar.

SELF-PORTRAIT

I walk between whitebrush and blackfoot
daisies alone at the desert botanical garden

and know not to touch the devil's
tongue or saguaro spines but still

I move my hand closer to the teddy bear
cholla until I touch it or it touches me

the needles clinging hollow
curve under the skin and I like it

I used to be a nice girl
euthymic too

but when the only thing
you have left of yourself
                          is pain

the filter with which
you move through

the world becomes impossibly
tender like fingers swollen

papules of foreign material
lodged in the body

to be unroofed or
left there to dissolve

SUPPOSE

you wake to sunshine on plastic patio furniture.
The smell of soft dirt fills your mouth.

Dragonflies hum over the lake
and the scalding dock

where you sit for hours, arms
tired from so much reaching.

You catch the long-bodied insect.
Its wings, translucent and veiny,

tickle the palms of your hands. You hold it
tighter, cupped and against your chest.

The heartbeat flutter of wings stops—
something only half-wished for.

WATCHING *LAW & ORDER: SVU* IN MY FATHER'S HOSPITAL ROOM

Stabler's alone
with a serial killer
who rapes and murders
prostitutes in the name
of his god. Guys like you,
you've always got a message.
It's cold. I move closer
to the window to feel the sun
on my left cheek, shoulder.
My father sweats out
the infection most
while asleep. We call
what happened a fluke,
an accident that not even
the best of detectives
could unravel, work
their way backwards
to a starting point
of which there is no
evidence, not even
a mark on his body
that says, Here,
it's going to happen.

/

On day one
he didn't know
who he was,
or where, or when.
He forgot how
to speak English.
Who am I? I asked.
No answer.
Quién soy?
Mi hija, he said.

/

I've seen this episode
before, already know
that the psychiatrist
father of the murdered boy
will kill his son's killer
when leaving the courtroom.
It's one of my father's favorites.
and even though he's asleep,
he knows how it ends,
knows that the father
will plead he was grief-
stricken and stand by his
professional opinion that
the sociopath would kill again
because even psychiatrists
know there are forces
in this world we cannot see
that for no reason
wish us harm.

/

The doctors tell us he is in the 1% of the 10% of the 100% which is to say
unlucky.

/

When we're alone,
I ask my father
my name, the date.
He tries but tires
quickly. Before he can
answer, his eyes
that are my eyes
close. I reach
for his hand,
his arm thinner
and bruised from when
he woke feverish
and pulled the second IV
from the hollow
crook of his elbow.

/

His breathing fluctuates
quietly as he does most things
these days. Benson and Stabler
play good cop, bad cop. I can tell
even when the volume's barely audible
that Olivia's the hard-ass—she paces
the interrogation room, stare fixed
on the alleged perps as she slams
her gun onto the steel table
between them, the veins in her neck
protruding and beautiful. Day four.
The nurse comes in to wake my father
for the third time today. And though
the voices on the screen are hushed,
I hit mute. She asks my father
his name, birthdate, what year we are in.
He looks to her then me after each answer,
eyes wide and waiting for confirmation.

MISSION BAY

I heard you're not dying anymore
though the last time we spoke

the words *blood-letting*
and *hemochromatosis* creeped

out of your mouth hesitant
as your I love you's

but you didn't hesitate when you
pointed your fingers shaped like a gun

at the bridge on Mission Bay you told me
about the time you were seventeen staring

at concrete slabs connecting land
and you dared your friend to jump in

to the cold bay waters
and the idiot broke his neck

not the way your body would break you
from the inside quietly

drowning itself in metallic
compounds that make blood

blood-colored and how red spilled
from the idiot's mouth agape

and you and the other boys ran
down steep steps to the bay-front

and swam to pull his limp body
shattered onto the sloped shore

though none of you knew
how to touch a broken thing

like I didn't know how
when I asked you years later

to let me help you and you told me
to let go and I didn't hesitate

not once to leave you broken
because what else could I offer

except words unable to fix you
or me because I can't help

but think of myself when I think of you
with your thick arm a needle a tube

connected to a machine taking from you
what we both knew I could not.

AUBADE

we lack a selvage
        somewhere in sleep
                our cells died

        bones and tissue pooled
in the mattress
        but we unravel

            at the margins
        unstitch the seams
until we've found

        fragments of flesh
            ready to be made
        whole again

careless undoers
        untanglers of threads
            we mend the frayed edges

        piece by piece
to a semblance
        of perfection

            this morning
        we fabricate each
other into being

E WATCHES MOTHER PRIMP

hair first
she blow-dries
fine strands
the perfect
amount
of volume
blonde
and never past
her shoulders
then makeup
a thin stroke
of liquid eyeliner
a few coats
of mascara
always lipstick
orange
with a hint
of pink
her breasts hang
a statue in pantyhose
trying on
dress after dress
stubborn
as a tongue
pressed
to the roof
of a mouth
shut tight
staring

MATH LESSON

You know you don't love him anymore
because you're not jealous of the woman

he's been staring at. She's a disco ball
sitting at the center of the restaurant

in her sequined blouse—polished and profound.
You bet she's good at tennis, or physics. You bet

she remembers the theory of special
relativity like she remembers to wear perfume.

You want him to spin her around
even though he's yours and it's your three-

year anniversary. You want anything
but for him to reach for your hand so you

grip the stem of your wine glass. Remember
jealousy is a matter of geometry—

it depends on where you place yourself
in relation to the other. Two people:

parallel lines. How long until
you touch him out of guilt or boredom?

PLAYING HOUSE

I've always taken my role seriously.
    In my sister's three-bedroom house,

    comfortable and bleached,
she gets to be the mom

and I pretend to sleep. Her husband's gone
    for the weekend on a hiking trip

    or retreat. Her son, the younger
of the two children, wakes

from hunger. She paces the room,
    a hand cradling his small frame,

    the other holding a bottle. It's okay,
it's okay, she says, a bounce

with each step. Mama's here,
    mama's here. I pretend I'm not

    listening, I don't hear.
When we were children

she'd say, I get to be the mom;
    my husband's at work. (The father

    was always working.) I'm older,
she'd say, you have to do what I want.

We'd play for hours in the closet
    under the stairs. She said babies

    don't walk, they don't talk, so I crawled
behind her not making a sound.

WATCHING *UNDERWORLD, INC.*
EPISODE 3: HUMAN CARGO

The Pima County Morgue,
approximately 110 miles

from my childhood home,
houses John Doe, Jane Doe,

[sexless] Doe. Dated remains
found in the Sonoran Desert—

nameless and alone. The medical
examiner holds a fragmented

cranium, points to where
the eyes would go.

/

I cross the border   on foot.
My father   waits for me

in the McDonald's   parking lot
one block   into America.

I stand in the line
labeled *Ciudadanos*.

            /

Francisco, a people smuggler
in Nogales, says his secret

is training others
to hide and survive.

/

I don't remember much from middle school
US History—   who lead the troops

that took   Fort Ticonderoga   or who forced
General Pemberton   to surrender in 1863—

but I remember like yesterday
the sound of my mother's voice

practicing   the Pledge of Allegiance
before her   naturalization ceremony.

/

A Border Patrol agent
explains how after five days

on foot in the desert,
skin begins to split

from the burning sun—
flesh exposed and open.

Nothing can be done once
the breaking has started.

/

Gratitude is a word that comes to mind.

/

In Phoenix, Magdalena buys and sells
moneyless migrants wholesale—

their families unable to pay off cartel
trafficking rates. Three women/girls sit

one room over, faces hidden with pillow cases—
they're background. And Magdalena, she talks

a tough talk, says business is business
and business is good. Her face concealed

by a black bandana and mirrored sunglasses
reflecting the camera back into itself.

/

When the show's over,   I'll call my mother
just to hear   the sound of her voice.

Como estas?   she'll ask.   And I'll lie,
tell her things are fine   the way

she'd say   the same to her mother
thirty years before   when she moved

to this country   alone
with her husband.   I'm haunted

by that for her.   I moved thousands of miles
away   alone   just to feel

closer. Before   we hang up, she'll say
Dios te bendiga,   picture me signing myself

or kissing a crucifix   I can't bring myself
to wear.   A blessing I don't need

but I take it   anyways.

AUTOCORRECT: NO SORROWS

mother here
you and I
is us
nosotros
(red underlined
incorrect)
left behind
in a place
only you
can call
your source
I am still
la gringa
unable to roll
my R's
ferrocarril
the tracks
rolling away
beside us
we drive north
the 95
winding through
slack roads
your home
to mine
distant as
the spanish
and english
in me
relentless
enemies
I am off-white
most days
with in be-
tween skin
mexicana in

me paled
by this
correction
nosotros be-
coming no
sorrows we
us you and I

WAITING WITH MY MOTHER IN THE CALIMAX PARKING LOT

Listening through the static of the radio,
a man sells divorces *sin dificultades*.

Mothers push children in shopping carts
across the pavement as the store empties,

each worn-out button on the dashboard
illuminated blue. We keep hush-hush

about certain things: how cellulite impregnates
the legs of women walking past the car;

that I don't like the saladitos Nana will buy
to lick out of halved oranges.

I don't tell Mother I know why Nana sleeps
in the living room—there's no point

in unmaking a bed for one.
Her diary reads *Ya no quiero vivir*.

Mother doesn't have to remind me:
it's unspoken, what we bear—

need in abundance.

NOTES

after Ocean Vuong

Most nights, I can't find the moon. This city's too flat. There are too many buildings.

Everyone in New England goes on and on about the smell of wet trees after rain. I prefer wet dirt in the desert.

New rule: never date a man whose favorite food is a turkey sandwich from Subway.

It's easy to confuse pity for anger.

I call my mother every day or else I'd go weeks without speaking Spanish here.

For the first three nights I stayed with him, I didn't brush my teeth or remove the black lining my eyes until morning.

Like any bad woman, I only like the beginnings of things.

How do I convince the white women at work that the A in my name isn't silent? If they mention The Plaza one more time, I'm going to lose it.

Sometimes I take off my glasses so my eyes can breathe.

Conversation in three text messages:
- I wish you could give me what I want.
- This isn't a great time to ask me for anything real. In fact, asking me for anything right now is complicated.
- I know.

This has always seemed temporary.

If he tries one more time to convince me that *I apologize* and *I'm sorry* are the same thing, I'm going to lose it.

I can tell how many days it's been since I've showered by the length of my armpit hair.

At a Christmas party, my grandmother's friend asked if I was the one who'd been chubby as a kid. I almost lost it.

Everything here deserves a picture.

I'm not a violent person. I'm not a violent person. I'm not a violent person.

Through an opaque curtain in the fast-fashion fitting room, I overheard a mother call her daughter a dumb bitch. I have it pretty good.

To buy: shampoo, hairspray, lotion, probiotics (capsules, not liquid)

Marasmus was a fun word to say until I looked it up.

I care so deeply about so little.

Things lost: my sex drive, his hair, our first apartment

In English, you say *I am afraid*. In Spanish, you say *I have fear*. I like that better.

I'm meant to be a person in the world not with him.

Current phobias: the dark, the number 4, colon cancer, being forgotten

What are you so afraid of, he asked.

Myself.

Everything.

In my experience, people don't invite you to stay until you're gone.

SELF-PORTRAIT

I'm dangerous;   there's little left
        inside this body—
that hasn't wanted   not to subtract
        from the world.

I can divide a man   into men. This
        isn't a warning
or confession.   Call me what
        you'd like;

in my own mind   I'm a mirror.
        I see everything
except myself.   This way I can't
        lose: even when

broken, a polished   surface reflects
        whatever looks in.

ACKNOWLEDGMENTS

Watching Underworld, Inc., Episode 3: Human Cargo is included in the Best New Poets 2017 anthology.

Thank you to the editors of the following journals in which poems from this collection first appeared, sometimes in slightly different versions or with different titles:

Bird's Thumb; The Boiler Journal; The Breakwater Review; Cherry Tree; Cider Press Review; The Cortland Review; Day One; Diode; Forklift, Ohio; Four Chamber Press; Gigantic Sequins; The Journal; Pittsburgh Poetry Review; Prelude Magazine; Public Pool; Queen Mob's Teahouse; The Rumpus; Synaesthesia Magazine; Tahoma Literary Review; TYPO; Vinyl; Word Riot.

Poems from this collection also appeared, sometimes in slightly different versions or with different titles, in the following chapbooks:
> *On Not Screaming*, Horse Less Press, 2016
> *Symptoms of Teething*, winner of the 2016 Vella Chapbook Prize, Paper Nautilus Press, 2017
> *Mexicamericana*, Pork Belly Press, 2017

Many thanks to Ada Limón for believing in these poems and helping them find a home. I'm greatly indebted to Adam Clay and Meagan Cass, my brilliant, patient, and thoughtful editors. To the Shelterbelt Press team and Brytton—thank you for your vision.

To my teachers: Jericho, Pablo, Maria, John—thank you for your guidance. Natalie, mil gracias.

To Kyle Dacuyan, my brother in words, with all my love. Always. To my friends for their unwavering support, especially: Jordan, Sarah J., Hanif, Jevon, Mandy, Sarah—thank you for letting me sleep on your couches, eat your food, and, above all, for your hugs when I've needed them the most. To Kassy, you often know me better than I know myself. Te quiero, prima.

Without my family, these poems would mean nothing. Lauro, Barbara, Barby, Isabella, Ryan, Emma, Max, and A—you are my everything. Los quiero, los adoro, son mi tesoro.

Thank you, reader. These poems are yours now.

Eloisa Amezcua is an Arizona native. Her
debut collection, *From the Inside Quietly*,
is the inaugural winner of the Shelterbelt
Poetry Prize selected by Ada Limón. She
is the author of three chapbooks and is
the founder and editor of *The Shallow
Ends: A Journal of Poetry*.